MOM, I FOUND A LUMP

By

GRAYCE UPSHAW

First published by AuthorHouse 07/30/04

ISBN: 1-4184-9236-1 (e-book)
ISBN: 1-4184-3330-6 (Paperback)

This book is printed on acid free paper.

Acknowledgments

There are so many people to thank that I almost hesitate to try, because I might inadvertently overlook someone.

First, my Bob, who makes every day a joy. He is as close to me as my next breath. He welcomed Kelly as his own, and it gave me such delight in seeing that relationship. My sons, Scott, deceased now, and Doug and Mac, still with us, who taught me that there is no greater reward in this life than being a Mom. To my sister, Kay, who has been a best friend to all of us. We are the last of our family, and our roots become more precious to us with each year that passes.

To the many, many friends and neighbors who came to help with their prayers, their donations, food, encouragement, and sometimes, just good ol' hugs! We treasure each and every one of you. Too many to name here. You do know who you are and we have already told you how much we love you.

To our friends at the Worship Center, especially Pastor Stan Hannan and Norma, who came into our lives just when we needed to be able to call on a Pastor, and we did(once at 6:30 a.m., sorry 'bout that!). Thanks for being there and for being good friends as well as Minister of the church we love.

To everyone who helped our Kelly in any way; there are so many to whom we are grateful. The people who cared for her at the hospitals and treatment centers and doctors offices, and George the druggist. Everyone who came into contact with her tried to make her day a little brighter. To Dr. Yandel, who treated Kelly respectfully, honestly and tenderly. We will always remember you. To her neighbors and friends who helped care for her, physically, emotionally, and spiritually, we will forever be grateful.

To John, thank you for giving our daughter 12, almost 13, years of unconditional love and the kind of life she had dreamed about as a little girl.

To Carol, who called me just before we made the trip for Kelly's funeral and told me that she was glad for the relationship that we all had. Thank you, Carol, and Lloyd(my ex-husband) for that relationship.

Along with her son, Kent, they were there to help and we all leaned on each other.

To sweet Lourdes, Mac's wife, thank you for being there for all of us and for bringing happiness to my "baby"

And finally, my publisher, 1ˢᵗ Books.

Dedication

To my surviving children, Doug and Mac, who have traveled this road with me twice, and who sometimes had to put their own grief aside for my sake.

These two tragedies eclipsed all other aspects of our life, but our shared strength and love for each other got us through it.

My greatest joy in life was being Mom to the four of you.

This is a story of relationships. I have not told it to make anyone feel sorry for me and it was certainly not my intention to elicit tears or sadness.

It is a story of mother and daughter, and how family members can support each other as they confront the worst blow ever dealt to them.

It is a story also, I hope, of communication.

The renowned Dr. Elizabeth Kubler-Ross, whose life study concerned the dying, believed and often said that the dying have unfinished business and cannot properly prepare to leave this world until it is done.

As we try to help those who are terminally ill, we find that they may have, conversely, helped us.

Thus this is a story of incredible bravery and strength.

If you are going through this now, or watching someone you love go through it, I hope you will find something in here to make those last days more meaningful.

Grayce Upshaw

Introduction

Mom, I found a Lump,

A story of survival, not of the loved one who lost the battle, but of the loved ones left behind. The telling of Kelly's story, from "Mom I found a lump" to the end of a beautiful life, takes the reader through an up-close-and personal Mother's view of the big "C". To her loved ones, their dear Kelly left a legacy of faith, bravery and courage that will never be forgotten.

By Pat Cavanagh, friend

Chapter One
June 29, 2001

The call came, like so many others, on an ordinary day. There was nothing to warn me as I absent-mindedly picked up my cordless white phone, that nothing would ever be ordinary again.

"Mom, I found a lump"

Did my heart really stop? How much time passed till it started beating again? The mother in me wanted to comfort my daughter and find the words to console her... to tell her that it was nothing and would soon go away. But as an R.N., I knew that the symptoms she was describing were serious indeed. Mentally, I quickly evaluated them, one by one: pain in the breast, pain down the arm, itching, night sweats, and weight loss of 5 pounds. How long had she been dealing with this?

"I just found it", she said, "I decided I'd better call you"

"Honey, I've never lied to you your whole life", I told her," This is not good. Make an appointment right away" Yes, she had a fair idea of what the next moves would be. She had grown up absorbing enough medical knowledge that people sometimes asked if she was also a nurse.

I think I must have known then the awful truth that was going to live among us for the next year and a half. After Kelly and I had talked for awhile, I hung up the phone and, as I waited for my husband, Bob, to come home from work, I thought a lot about our Kelly. Our Kelly. My oldest child and only daughter. Bob is her stepfather, but Kelly was quick to tell you that he was her "daddy". She was 19 when Bob and I met and 21 when we married, young enough to accept him as a parent and old enough to form a friendship with him as an adult. They had a special bond and each was always there for the other. They shared a love of sports and especially enjoyed watching football together, though they might cheer for opposing teams. Having had three brothers, Kelly understood the ins and outs of the game. She was way ahead of me. She and Bob tried, but I just didn't get it and still don't.

She and John had been married about 2 years when Bob had his heart bypass surgery in 1992. Kelly went to her boss and said, simply "John and I need some time off, my stepfather is having surgery." She said she knew she didn't need to ask John, there was no question that this was where they both would want to be.

Kelly was an organizer, the kind of young woman who would take charge of things, the kind of friend who would bring a meal when you were sick and who would bring little gifts for all the kids if you had a new baby. By becoming a wife and mother Kelly had fulfilled every dream she had had growing up. She loved being John's wife, loved being Mom to Anthony and Meghan, and was very contented with her house and her life. Her accounting business, run from home, was doing well, she had wonderful, long-time friends, and up till now their only problem had been that Anthony, 5, had ADHD(attention deficit hyperactive disorder)

This situation could be very difficult at times, but Kelly never doubted for a minute that this was the life she wanted. She and John were lucky to have found each other and they both knew it. And so did we.

She and John had met while she was working as an accountant and he as an engineer for the same large company in Melbourne, Florida. I think from the first moment they met they realized that they were meant to be together. They never ran out of things to talk about, she said. They both had a love of the outdoors and were married in a small mountain-top ceremony in Colorado in 1990.

She was the type of person you knew you could trust with your secrets. She didn't need to be the center of attention, but very often was because people were drawn to her. She knew how to be a friend... a best friend..

I sat there quite awhile, waiting for Bob to come home, and thought about the all night Monopoly or Balderdash games with her brothers, the times she helped out in our Hardware store and simply had a ball doing it. "Don't let this change", I thought, "Don't let this be what I think it is"

When Bob came in we just held each other and tried not to say it, tried not to think it.......but we both knew..............................

3

From the first day Bob came to my house in 1978 and met my children he showed them respect, and a genuine interest in who they were and what they were about. Two years later we were married and our life as a family began.

From the ceramic projects on the dining room table, on through the years to the cooking contests, guitar competitions, boyfriend problems, school functions, homework, proms, emergency rooms, and yes, discipline, Bob was there to provide assistance, affirmation, guidance. Yes, I had laid the foundation before. They had learned about honesty and kindness and that I was always available to them and we could talk about anything and everything, but now they had that inestimable male presence to fill in the gaps, to teach the things I couldn't know about; "manspeak" with the boys as they learned about sports, and fixing things, and how to treat girls, and for Kelly, bonding of a special sort, the only girl at last finding the place in her special male's life that daddies save for their daughters. They were buddies, they were confidantes, they teased each other, they helped each other, and now, her every pain was felt by him.

Chapter Two
July, 2001….. Biopsy

We've all met lousy doctors. I still wonder at the first one Kelly encountered (her first choice was out of town.) After a cursory exam, and pretty much ignoring the symptoms, he told her it was probably an infection….an infection he did not attempt to treat.

Statistically, most lumps prove to be benign but there are times when that inner voice must be heard. Further investigation was warranted. Needless to say, Kelly went right from this doctor to someone closer to the top of his class in medical school This doctor knew that something needed investigating and he sent her straight to a surgeon.

As quickly as all of this was handled, precious days still went by. It was with some alarm that Kelly and John observed visible signs that the something was growing…..and growing fast. Also, the left breast area was warm to the touch, and the skin was rippling .

While this was going on, Bob and I were at home, waiting for further word and I was trying to convince myself that God would not be so cruel as to take another child from me. Twelve years before, our middle son, Scott, had been killed in a motorcycle accident. No, please God, I can't do that again!

A biopsy of the breast and of the lymph nodes was immediately scheduled. We sat in the waiting room trying to be of comfort to John, and trying to read, as people have done for years in waiting rooms, but our eyes kept going to that operating room door every few minutes, to see if the next time it opened it would be the doctor we were waiting for.

And, finally, out he came, his otherwise pleasant face showing the strain of having had to deliver bad news too many times. Yes, it was cancer and it had already invaded the lymph nodes. A few weeks later further testing would show that it was not in the abdomen or the bones. It was, however, a fast-growing cancer and was advancing rapidly.

We agonized over the logistics of getting her somewhere for treatment ; should we send her to the cancer center in Houston, Texas, and have her stay with her dad and stepmother? But that would mean being away from her husband and two little ones with no chance for them to visit. Should we try to get her in at the Moffett Cancer center in Tampa? Could we get them back and forth?

Should we bring her to our home in Ft. Lauderdale and try to get her back and forth to Miami, 25 miles away, for treatment?

And what about John and the children? While Meghan was only 2 and independent enough to fare pretty well during times of change, Anthony, at 5 years of age, did not respond at all well to any variation in his regular routine. This is one of the earmarks of ADHD.

The matter was settled for us by.....we should have known..... the insurance company. They would not authorize any plan we were considering. Kelly would have her treatment right in her own home town. In the inexplicable way that these things sometimes happen, it turned out to be just short of a miracle.

Her doctor insisted that she begin chemotherapy as soon as it could be arranged. He scheduled her with an Oncologist, who had trained at the Moffett center in Tampa, and he was wonderful! The care that she has received has been phenomenal. The people in every office have been knowledgeable, efficient, compassionate; one could not ask for more. Kelly has trusted them to care for her and they have, giving her an affection that helped her to feel less alone when we couldn't be there.

"Mom, I know I have it, but I just can't bring myself to say the word"

"I know, Honey, try not to think of it that way. This is going to be the biggest battle of your life. Think of it that way, a big fight. Can you just get mad and say "F—- you? F—— you, cancer, I am not going to let you get me!"

She gave me an impish grin, and referring back to those oh-so-rebellious teen years, said "Why not? I've said it to you often enough!" One of the few laughs that came our way …and we grabbed it and held on to it as tightly as we held on to each other!

Chapter three
About Kelly

This is as good a place as any to tell you about Kelly as a young girl, and to describe, if I can, the qualities that defined her as a woman. Maybe I can't. Can I transport memories to the written word and familiarize you with the essence that was Kelly? Such a sweet precious, little girl, very personable, and very bright, and she loved to read! Back when she was little we would ride in the car and read the business signs that we passed. We played the usual child games, but found much more entertainment from books. Kelly, and her brothers to follow, would all rather go to a bookstore than a candy store. She was a very strong, spirited, smart, loving creature. As she grew, her characteristics of compassion and loyalty manifested themselves more prominently, as well as some feistiness.

She had a tender heart and would care for anyone who needed it but could fight with the best of them for a cause she believed in. And the mouth! Her three brothers would get into trouble and take their punishment and go on, but Kelly always had to compound hers with the fresh mouth….and she ended up getting more restriction time added. I always knew deep down that this strength would help her to cope with the world in adulthood, but nonetheless it made for an interesting, challenging adolescence.

She loved to cook and had, from early childhood, had her own utensils and whatever dish I prepared, she would be putting some in her own little pots and pans, right alongside me. She became an excellent, enthusiastic cook. In later years she and I would make large platters of every kind of cake and cookies and breads and deliver them to friends and neighbors at Christmastime. After she and John were married in Colorado in 1990 we had a huge reception at our home and Kelly and I prepared all the food, including the 3 –tiered wedding cake with the champagne glasses and rings and doves which had been on an identical cake that I had made for Scott. As he had passed away the year before, Kelly had requested this cake and I was only too happy to oblige.

Her first job as a teenager had been at a Dairy Queen and she budgeted her paychecks and managed to save a little money, even lent some to friends. No one ever failed to pay her back. She was a tremendous help to me in raising the boys, as I had to work, and often took extra hospital shifts for supplemental income.

With one paycheck she went shopping at the Mall and returned with a nice little inexpensive Bulova watch for me. "This is a 'just because' gift", she said." I just realized that all you've ever had is Timex work watches"

I remember a day when I came home to find the house clean and orderly, but with throw pillows and other items in the wrong places. I thought no more about it till some time later when I learned that my two older sons and some of their friends had decided to skip school and party at my empty house. Kelly came home unexpectedly, found them there, made them clean up, and then called every single parent with the message "I'm calling to tell you where your kid was today when you thought he was in school"

When I learned about this I asked why she never told me any of it.

"Mom you had enough to worry about. I handled it"

Things were far from perfect. There was very little money and there was a lot of stress. Even as this person of integrity and wholesomeness was forming, the rebellious teenage spirit surfaced often. I would learn later that she and her buddy, Samantha (Sam) used to skip school and go "pool hopping", scaling fences to swim in the pool of their choosing. I didn't know about this at the time.

I did learn that Kelly had skipped school one other time. I had given her permission to go to "Gator Growl", a big football event at the college her current boyfriend attended. She was to have her car serviced and run some errands for me and I would let the school know that she was out with my permission. Before this could take place I received a call from the school telling me that Kelly had already skipped 2 days.

"Well, Kelly, I thought we had a deal and that I could trust you. Apparently you've already taken your holiday so now you don't get to go to Gainesville for Gator Growl"

You can imagine the furor that this caused! There was a lot of screaming and crying. Everyone who knew her came to plead with me on her behalf; her brothers, her friends, the boyfriend. I even began to question myself at this point, but my mother's words, a creed that we lived by, came back to me. "You don't have to agree with what I say, but you do have to be able to trust me when I say it"

She did not go to Gator Growl. I was a pretty tough parent, not so much in later years, but I had to be then. Many years later she would admit that she knew I did the right thing, even when it happened.

"I knew you were right, Mom, but I thought it was worth a try to talk you out of it"

Mealtimes were not allowed to be interrupted. Anyone who called or came by was told to come back later. When Kelly was in her thirties and she and John were making application to become foster parents, she would list this as one of her favorite childhood memories. We did then, and still do, sit around the table after our meal, sharing our thoughts, coming together. Sometimes we will sit for ½ hour or more. We played all sorts of board games and card games, where my favorite part would be watching Kelly and her brothers teasing each other as only siblings can.

I don't know how or when Kelly became our Santa Claus but it was she who always distributed the gifts on Christmas day. There is still a gaping hole in that spot now.

There was no way I could have sent a kid away to college, and Kelly started night school on her own, taking class after class and working at the same time. It took her several years, but she got her B.S.

degree, made the Dean's list, and proudly gave me a photocopy for her baby book.

Shortly before Bob and I got married we had had a minor spat and I was having a hard time pulling myself together for work the next morning, after a sleepless night. Kelly brought me a cup of tea with the admonition" Have you forgotten that I'm not just your daughter, I'm your friend? Do you want to talk?" Later that day my beeper went off and there she was. "You were so upset this morning, I just wanted to see how you're doing"

Her childhood friends remained her friends for all of her life. No matter how many new ones came, there were one or two from Girl Scout days who still counted her among their best friends. She knew how to be a friend, to be supportive, to be there, to be interested in where your life was taking you. Now she was down and her many acts of kindness to others would soon be coming back to her.

Chapter Four
August, 2001 Chemo

Chemo(chemical)therapy is the delivery of chemicals into the system, deadly chemicals, hopefully powerful enough to overcome the cancer. There are several drugs used :Cytoxan, Methotrexate, Cytoxan, Fluorouracil, Adriamycin are a few. There are more. Because each attacks a different stage in the life cycle of a tumor, combinations of these are used much more effectively than any one by itself..

A port was inserted into the large subclavian vein in Kelly's chest, just under the collarbone. This is a surgical procedure, done under anesthesia, but necessary because none of the small arm veins normally used to deliver medication could withstand the assault of the delivery of these caustic agents.

Kelly tolerated this procedure rather well but the port would always be an annoyance in her chest.

We traveled there for this procedure.

I had watched her being wheeled to the OR several times during her childhood, but this was different.

Now we were officially engaged in a most dreaded battle. The battle against cancer had begun.

The tumor was Grade III, Stage III, indicating that it had already migrated beyond its original site and that it was very serious, grade IV and Stage IV being the worst. While there is a 90% plus cure rate with most breast cancers, Kelly's was an inflammatory type, rare, fast-growing and very aggressive, demanding an equally aggressive treatment. Chemo began, the strongest dose they could use. For the next four days there was non-stop nausea and vomiting and weakness so debilitating that Kelly couldn't lift her head off the pillow. Her hair fell out...almost all of it. Her mouth was a mass of sores; eating was painful, if not impossible.

How do I describe the helpless feeling of seeing my child go through this and wishing it could be me instead? How to describe the agony of wondering if it would work at all?

"I know I have to lose the breast, Mom, but I hate being bald just as much"

"I know honey, I wish I could make all this go away"

"I know I'm going to beat this, Mom, but you know what I'm most afraid of?

"What?"

"I'm afraid it'll come back in a year or 5 or 10, or sometime when I least expect it"

This is the time when you don't search for words...there are none. This is the time when you just hold out your arms and offer what comfort you can.

The next two chemos actually went rather smoothly. An adjustment in the anti- nausea medication helped a lot, and there was minimal nausea. Kelly's appetite was very good, and, for the first time in her life, long, hard, lovely fingernails began to grow. Go figure! The investment was made in the traditional turbans and hats but she stubbornly refused to surrender the last few wisps of hair and shave her head.

We were burning up the roads, trying to be there as much as we could. In addition, our youngest son, Mac, drove up to accompany her on her weekly chemo appointments. This pleased us so much! He did it to enable us to have a break, but he was also able to offer her a type of companionship that no one else but a brother can. So many times I gave thanks that she was such good friends with her two brothers. Our older son, Doug, was on a brand new job in another state, and unfortunately, unable to come here. He had, however, offered to have Kelly move in with him and she could have her treatments in the large, well-known center in Atlanta, near to where he lived. Each of our children, so individual, each with different strengths, different approaches to life. Kelly a fairly typical female in that she was "out there" with her feelings. The boys, fairly typical males in their keep-it-inside-try-not-to-let-it-show. Strong, capable, and supportive nonetheless, we only saw the raw edges of their suffering.

Chapter Five

We settled into a sort of routine. Mac went up when she had her treatments, which usually left her feeling extremely tired. She could no longer walk unassisted and continued to lose precious pounds. My husband, Bob, and I would go for some of the treatments, or in between, and many other times when things took a downward turn, as they often did.

When we weren't there, she was well-cared for by the best of friends. We are still amazed at the lengths to which people have gone in order to help our daughter.

One friend picked up Anthony at school and took him to join Meghan at daycare so John could pick them both up when he got off work. The babysitter, sweet, caring, long-time friend Candy, sent home dinner every night.

Tiny, blonde, a composite of energy and calm, her stature belies her stamina. A few years back, Candy had resigned from the company where she and Kelly and John had all been co-workers in order to become a full time caregiver to a handful of children. Anthony before her, and now Meghan, had found a second home with Candy.

There were other friends who kept the children on weekends, did housecleaning or sent grocery gift certificates and other items, saying they were sorry they couldn't be there to actually fix the meal. Most people will never go through something like this but if you do I hope that you will be embraced and surrounded with as much caring and compassion as we were.

One friend, Carlotta, came every day for months, making sure that Kelly got her shower, her meals, and that she did NO housework. This friend kept the laundry caught up, tidied up the house, and chauffeured Kelly to the doctor, or wherever she needed to go. She ran errands, picked up prescriptions, you- name-it! How in the world can you ever thank someone for doing all that?

The physical resemblance between Carlotta and Kelly was remarkable. Both were slightly built, wore glasses for reading, very little makeup, and had almost the same shade of light brown hair. They could even wear each others' clothes and were sometimes mistaken for sisters, a fact which made them both giggle with pleasure. Carlotta brushed off any attempt to thank her for any act of kindness. "She's my friend", she would say "she would have done the same for me"

And how lucky she was to have John! He shared every aspect of this with her and tried to make it easier in any way he could. When we went up there we went for him as well as for Kelly. On one trip we sent him off with Bob for an afternoon of fishing and then to a sports bar for some R &R. They came home giggling and silly and for a few hours the worry lines weren't so evident on John's face. We felt that was all we could do for him, till his wife and his life were returned to him. We were so grateful that our daughter had him. When Kelly first met him and she told us about him she said" Mom, the best thing I can say about him is that he's just like Bob"

Enough said…………………

Things were under control. When Kelly telephoned with one of those "I need you" calls, we grabbed the already-packed bag, and left. One of these calls came because a small hole had eaten its way into the breast, "about the size of a dime," she said. The doctor wanted Kelly to change her bandages twice a day and pack the wound with saline dressings, wet to dry. This was very distasteful to her and I was going up to help with it. I decided to go alone and encouraged Bob to stay behind. After all, he still worked three days a week and I didn't. Both Bob and my sister, Kay, tried to talk me out of it but I was only going to be gone a day or two….no big deal.

I'm an old E.R. nurse. I have seen kids blown apart, brains splattered about, drowning, partial decapitations, but this was my kid! I saw that the breast was pretty much eaten away.

"Kelly, I thought you said this was the size of a dime!?"

"Well, yesterday, it was. The doctor says the chemo is eating the healthy tissue as well as the bad. I can't look at it"

Well, the dressings went well, she actually had mastered it even without looking at it; I only needed to guide her. When the time came for me to leave I got as far as the corner and totally "lost it". I know now what "racking sobs" are. I did this all the way home…three hours on the turnpike. Never have I experienced a feeling like seeing part of my child being eaten away.

Chapter Six
Support of friends and family

We have experienced every emotion there is during this ordeal; fear, anxiety, protectiveness, hopelessness, helplessness, despair, gratitude. The full range.......

While this story isn't about me, I should mention here the tremendous support system that I have had as well. Bob and I are members of a wonderful church where we have many friends, and even some that we don't know as well called to put Kelly on their prayer list or just to inquire about how she was doing or to offer whatever they could. Our friends and neighbors, the best in the world, kept us going and offered everything they could, right down to transportation for the three hour trip if ever it was needed.

Just before all this began we had planned a move out of the big city to a small town about 5 hours drive from here. We thought we wanted to live a simpler life. There are many reasons why this didn't work out, and maybe we'll never be sure what force it was that pulled us back at the last minute, but we know that it happened just short of putting the deposit on the house and having it be irrevocable.

We are so glad that we did pull back. We have the kind of neighbors and friends that couldn't ever be replaced and we don't know how we would have gotten through the last few months without the love and concern and prayers and help of all kinds that have been and still are offered to us.

This is a time when good-times only acquaintances will separate themselves from true no-matter-what friends. You find new, valuable friends in places you never planned on and, sadly, some you thought were like family sometimes make themselves scarce. In our old neighborhood we had one such couple as neighbors. They had been in our home off and on through the years for the fun times but couldn't even walk across the lawn to offer us a word of comfort when Scott died in 1989. As soon as it became undeniably clear that they were not friends, I never again tried to tell myself that they were. This is a very painful lesson. All I can tell you is don't waste your energy crying over those people. You will need it for too many other things. The many many other people who come forward to let you know they care will render the others insignificant.

Our lives were put on hold. We couldn't make any plans; we were always on the alert to make that trip if a setback occurred, and there were some. When we were at home, our minds were still up there with her.

When I talk about support systems I have to tell you here that only if you have a sister will you understand this next part. A sister is that someone who knows you like no other, who is there in your corner when you need her. Whatever the need she's there. Even if there should be times when her brain may tell her that you are wrong, her heart always tells her that she is 100% on your side, ready to help, to advise, to comfort, to work alongside you, or merely listen.

Bob and I are lucky to have my sister as a best friend to both of us. She has been an integral part of the children's' lives as they were growing up, also, and still is. I give thanks every day for her, and for Bob, the best husband that God ever put on this earth. I could go on and on about this but will instead say that every part of my life has been better for having him in it. The good parts are twice as good and the bad parts only half as bad, because he shares them with me. He came into my life when I had been a divorced parent for 3 years. When we were married two years later he became a father to my four kids, all of whom would walk through fire for him. They adore him, as I do.

If this is beginning to sound too "Donna Reed", let me assure you now, that it was not all smooth sailing. There were many problems along the way; some were solved, some still have not been.

One such was a nurse who shall remain nameless.

Chapter Seven
A lesson in unkindness

On one of her hospital admissions, Kelly was a little more apprehensive than usual, for she was not going to the Same Day Surgery Center where the people and the routine were familiar. Instead, she had to go to the large, impersonal regional medical center for this surgery. "Don't worry, honey", I told her, confidently, "There will be one nice person, that's all you need, one nice person who will take you by the hand and make you feel less afraid. After that it gets easier" I would have to eat those words.

No one said a kind word to her from the time the nurse's aide began the "cattle call" in the lobby" Okay, everyone up to the second floor!" Kelly was then shown to a stretcher behind a curtain, with still no one uttering a word to her. Now the reality was beginning to hit her and the "one nice person" wasn't in evidence.

The nurse who was assigned to her stood behind Kelly's back and was facing me across the stretcher, silently handing Kelly a gown and then issuing instructions. Kelly now began to sob in earnest. I held her, and, facing the nurse over her shoulder, said "She's nervous. Her husband couldn't be here and it was kind of a cattle call downstairs. She's having a bad time" The response was" When it's this busy, that's the only way we can do it"

Now Kelly began to really want to bolt out of this place and I wanted to smack this self-righteous, unfeeling, obviously misplaced excuse for a caregiver. Instead I composed myself for Kelly's sake and said "My daughter has cancer, she's in a lot of pain, and she's frightened. I am not just a hysterical mother I am an R.N. and I know how this is supposed to go" Still no reply. There would not be anyone to speak kindly to my daughter until 40 minutes after her arrival when the anesthesiologist came in. Later this nurse would tell my daughter that I "came down on her". "No", said Kelly. "I've seen my mother come down on people. If she had you would have known it!"

Fortunately two nurses, one male and one female, stayed with Kelly through surgery and recovery and gave her all the comfort and assistance and reassurance that I had promised her and that EVERY patient should have a right to expect.

When all of this settled down, I wrote a letter to the hospital administrator, urging that their help and their routine be re-evaluated. If this was the best that they could offer perhaps this nurse needed to consider another area.

Kelly also wrote a letter urging them to take a good look at their routines, for some of their patients may be coming for the first time and would think that this was standard procedure! This nurse somehow obtained Kelly's phone number and called her at home! This is, by the way, very much against the rules and the privacy laws. She thought we were trying to make her lose her job.

"No", said Kelly, "I only wanted you to DO your job, and you weren't" Good nurses are hard to find and it was never our intention to have her fired, but if she needed to be reassigned, then do so, for everyone's sake. We were both gratified to receive replies from the hospital, assuring us that they have redone their admission procedures and generally made the whole process more humane. After reviewing my credentials, outlined in my letter, the administrator was convinced that I was not just a mother yelling because her kid was hurt and she had the good sense to re-evaluate and make changes where needed. The nurse in question is in another area, we don't know the whole story. She could have been prosecuted for calling Kelly at home, but I do feel that my daughter may have actually saved her job. This lady was headed for trouble sooner or later. And I was, once again, proud of the way my Kelly handled things.

Chapter Eight

Not once did I hear Kelly ask "Why me?" At every stage she bravely said, "Whatever I have to do I'll do it"

Her brother, Mac, once asked her how she could go through it without complaint; the brutal chemotherapy, the surgeries, the constant pain, the humiliation of the procedures, and she simply replied" I have a family. That's all that matters"

I asked "why her?" many times.

I remembered her first steps, her first word, her first date. Now it was the first time seeing her baldness, the first time seeing pain that I couldn't alleviate, the first time seeing fear that no one could make go away. As always, Carlotta was there when John couldn't be and there were many others who offered help also. These many acts of thoughtfulness were so much appreciated by us, as we knew that she was in good hands when we couldn't be there.

When we were there we faced some different problems, some logistic, some not in our ability to solve. Since Kelly's illness Anthony had become increasingly more difficult and wanted everything to be done only by Mommy and Daddy. It took every ounce of energy that Kelly had even to fix a drink for one of the children and it broke our hearts to watch, but that was the way it was. Most of the burden naturally fell to Daddy (John) This severely limited our options. In the beginning we took the two kids back and forth, ran errands, etc. (we actually put 142 miles on the car in one day) Now we could only pick Anthony up at school but couldn't take him in the morning. He wanted Daddy to do that.

When his medication wore off it was beyond our ability to handle. Tantrums were frequent, meals were impossible, and sleep was out of the question. The children didn't settle down till very late, and before morning at least one had gone into Kelly and John's bed. John very often had to go to the Florida room or into one of the children's' rooms to finish out the night. If Bob and I were there, he and I would share a small open-out sofa in the living room, or I would take that and he would have the slippery leather sofa in the Florida room. With all of the late hours and traffic during the night no one slept. We just found that a motel was the best answer if anyone was to be able to function next day.

Meghan, age two, became more difficult to handle as well. Much as we wanted to be of help in this area we found that we simply couldn't. In the uncanny way that kids have, they knew that something was going on, and in the uncanny way that kids have, they chose the worst time to act out....the time when we were all exhausted and vulnerable. Only John was up to the challenge. We did the usual and expected cooking, and picking up, etc. only sometimes able to give a kid a bath or play a game for awhile.

We worried a lot about John and tried to help Kelly focus on getting well. Much as we loved our grandchildren, we couldn't do much to relieve John of the burden except to take the children for walks or play with them in the yard for awhile.

Back at the motel we always felt frustrated and helpless, wishing that we could do more.

Chapter Nine

When Kelly's white blood cell counts dropped frighteningly low or if she developed an infection, Carlotta, ten minutes away, always made herself available and was at the hospital with her even as we were grabbing the always-ready bag and locking our front door. Normal white cell count is between 5,000 and 10,000. Chemotherapy, unfortunately, can take these to dangerously low levels, necessitating the temporary suspension of the life-saving treatment. This is a very precarious position to be in. Kelly's count often dropped as low as 500!

She was on every prayer list in our state, I think. People who didn't even know her became acquainted in the various waiting rooms and each would end up wanting to pray for the other and to hope for each other's recovery.

Although not his biological daughter, Kelly is very much Bob's "little girl" and this has been very hard on him. I had met him 23 years before, just a few months after his first wife had died of breast cancer. Kelly had dreaded telling him her diagnosis because she didn't want him to have to deal with this once again. He was always ready to jump in the car and go, if she needed us or to just 'be there" as often as we could. It wasn't always because she asked. Sometimes he would just sense that she needed us and, truthfully, sometimes it was our need to just be near her.........

There were some lighter times. We tried to keep our humor whenever possible, and however small the opportunity. Kelly had learned that there were only two plastic surgeons in her area; one was 25 miles away and the one who would most likely do her reconstructive surgery was….guess what? A hand specialist!

"Guess what, Mom? A hand specialist is going to reconstruct my boobs!"

"Well, honey, I'm sure he's very good. So you'll just have a thumb and two fingers hanging off your chest!"

Like I said, we took our laughs wherever we could find them……………..

In November, as she awaited radiation, reconstructive surgery, and maybe more chemo, the Oncologist said that he would like her to have the surgery early in December. Kelly wanted to have the surgery a little later, so that she could go to John's company party. She wanted to get all dressed up in a gown, wear makeup, dance, and party hearty! We understood that. For one night she wanted to forget what was ahead. To live like she used to. To live like she wanted to again. To have a magic night with John before the surgeon and the oncologist took over her life again.

All we could say was:

Do it!

Yes!

You go girl!!!!!!!!

Chapter Ten
December, 2001
The Mastectomy

The mastectomy went well; so well, in fact, that we didn't need to go up there. "Mom, you know there's nothing I'd like more than to have you here, but I'll need you more afterward, when John goes back to work". Okay, that made sense. He was having a hard time getting enough hours in to draw his full salary every week. We wanted to be there the night before to give her a hug, and offer some support, but she was right. In addition, we were run down, and unknowingly, fighting off viral infections that were soon to knock us flat and wipe away any Christmas spirit that might have been. Our annual party had been canceled. We had planned nothing, because we couldn't, with any certainty. Christmas was to be very simple and last minute, and truth be told, none of us had the holiday spirit anyway. We didn't feel like shopping, either. We decided on a very quiet celebration with minimal gifts. Since there had always been the possibility of having to be away during the holidays, we had not even planned to put up the tree, but recanted at the last minute, and did, in fact, have a beautiful, if simple, holiday. Since becoming a mother, Kelly had decided, just as I had as a young mother, that Christmas would now be a stay-at-home holiday for them. They usually came for a visit either just before or just after, but we didn't spend the actual day together. We missed her a lot at this time, but also knew that we could be infectious to her if we visited, and so had to wait. This was not a happy time.!

Kelly, meanwhile was doing very well!. John, who never questioned or resisted anything that had to be done, changed her bandages. When you read about some of the husbands who can't look at their wives after this surgery, or worse, just pack up and leave, you wonder how they could be so cruel to someone already so vulnerable. It was never an issue with any of us. Kelly knew, we all knew, that she never had to give a thought to how John would handle this. After a couple of days she looked at the surgical site herself "Well, if it's gone, it's gone..life goes on!" Kelly was about 5'7 ½ and very slim. She found John's shirts loose and comfortable, and joked that anyone who saw her hairless head and lanky body in her husband's shirts had better not call her "sir!"

Mac went up frequently, either spending the night, or coming back the same day. He would do the laundry and whatever chores needed to be done, take her to chemo, take her to lunch when she was able, and just be there for her to talk to and to hold onto.

"Mom, when did Mac get to be my 'big brother'?"

"I have no idea, sweetie, but isn't it nice?"

When Mac was born, Kelly was 9 years old, feeling very "motherly" and quite taken with him. I had come home from the hospital too early and was not up and about very much, and Kelly was only too willing to help out with this new little person. Now he was caring for her, much to her delight.

The nurses and staff at the treatment center were impressed with her fighting spirit and amazed by her attitude."I lived 42 years before this hit me and I plan to live another 42 years. This is just a blip on the radar screen!"

Then news of her positive attitude soon spread.

"Mom, they want me to go around and talk to groups, and to patients who have this thing, like I do"

"Yes, honey, I do see you as an advocate. You have touched a lot of people"

" But I don't want to talk about it. Once I'm done with all this treatment, I don't ever want to talk about it or think about it again"

"UmmmHmmmmmmmmmmmm We'll see…………………."

Our first time up there, we were delighted to see things going so well. She was progressing nicely and having minimal pain. Things were under control, but she was weak and in bed a lot. This didn't seem out of the ordinary for a post-op. We went home feeling pretty good about things…..until the headache came.

In January she started to complain that her headache wouldn't go away. She was staying in the bedroom with the shades drawn because the light bothered her. It was difficult to keep food down because of the nausea. There was a family history of migraine headaches on her dad's side of the family, but this didn't quite fit the pattern because it didn't come and go, as migraines do. With all of her cat scans and other tests coming back negative the doctors determined that muscle spasm was the culprit. Lying in bed all the time had caused it.

We drove up to take her to an appointment with a masseuse, as ordered, and while this did help some, it did not address the problem. Watching the pain when she turned her head gave us a clue that something was very horribly wrong here. Bob and I agonized over this.

"I know that all the tests are negative, but all it takes is one little cell to break loose and go traveling"

Bob's response was a quiet "I know, Honey", which was muffled by my crying as he held me and we both thought the unthinkable.

Kelly was hospitalized for further tests.

Chapter Eleven
Metastasis

On Valentine's day Bob and I waited early in the morning to talk to the doctor. John had asked that we do this so that he could get the kids off to school and get in some work time He was having a hard time getting his full schedule in at work. He would come to the hospital later in the day. Kelly's oncologist, sober-faced, met us outside her room. We had been watching the fish swim aimlessly in the aquarium at the end of the hall by her room and now we felt as adrift as they seemed. He began his report with "The news couldn't be worse". The cancer had now metastasized from the breast to the meninges, the covering of the brain and spinal cord. It had an ugly name: Carcinomatous Meningitis. Prognosis: 6 to 12 months! In just 7 months she had reached a stage that usually takes much longer. Now we knew what hell was, and despair and fear. We were shocked and horrified…but not surprised. This is one of the times when being an R.N. is a very weighty thing. Too much knowledge and all that.

Part of being an R.N. is being able to see past the doctor's professional demeanor to the pain beneath when all of the knowledge and skill may not be enough. This esteemed Oncologist, dear Dr. Yandel, had sat at Kelly's bedside with her, swapping stories about their families, camping and other similar interests, as their respective children were fairly close in age. He always met with us and kept us informed and included in her care, and was not too proud to throw in a hug now and then.

We had waited in the waiting room downstairs for John in order to give him the news in the gentlest way possible, before he went in to see Kelly. We waited near the gift shop, and I thought "We could buy Kelly every gift in there, but can't give her the one gift that she needs!"

We wanted him to get there quickly so that this chore could be behind us, but at the same time, we were almost glad for the delay, because in the telling, the dreaded prognosis would become profoundly true.

John came in, looking straight ahead and surprised to see us in the lobby but, as awareness spread over his face, not too surprised to hear what we had to tell him. While we all did our crying in that waiting room that had seen so many tears before, we once again realized how lucky she was to have him. "I don't want her to suffer", he said". If they can't prolong her life, I don't want her to suffer" Our thoughts exactly.

Tall, bearded, quietly self-assured, one might at first think of John as serious, but oh, he and Kelly knew how to have fun together, whether it was screaming at the plays during a football game, or working in the yard. They complemented each other so well and were true partners. They knew how to work together, to play together, and to respect each other. When she was still single, Kelly and I had talked often about staying in love and the equal importance of staying in "like". I had wished for her, for all my children, to find what Bob and I had and she knew that she had. Every wish she had had as a girl growing up, had come true in her life with John and the children.

When Kelly was told the news by her doctor, her response was "No way"

"I have two children", she said, "I'm not leaving here in six months!"

We all gathered around her bed and tried to comfort her and each other as she courageously agreed to whatever gruesome plan they came up with in order to prolong her life...and gruesome it would be.

Calling the rest of the family was extremely difficult. We had lost our son, Scott in 1989, from a motorcycle accident, and none of us was prepared to go through that kind of grief again. Kelly was my oldest child and only girl, and very close to her brothers. They took this news very hard, as did her Aunt, my sister.

"Kay, I want you to sit down and I'll tell you what's happening. Is there someone there with you?"

"No, my neighbor just left"

"The news isn't good. I'll tell you everything, and then I want you to call someone to come and stay with you"

As we cried together we were both sorry that she had not made the trip with us. It was very tough for her to be there by herself, and to hear this over the phone.

"I know one thing, you'd better not ever move away. It's lonely here without you. Are you all right?"

"Yes, I can't let myself go yet. If I do I won't stop. It just doesn't seem real I can't bury another child, I just can't!" As I made the many calls which were to be made, translating the 'doctorspeak" as I did, I heard myself saying things that sounded as if they were being said by someone else. Am I really telling people that my Kelly has metastatic cancer and may have only a few months left????

Bob and I tried to be strong for everyone else, a point noted by our oldest son, Doug.

"Mom, you shouldn't be making these calls; you have us. Let us do this" He was there to help and he was right. Doug had been our mainstay when we owned our business and had been there to help during Bob's heart surgery and whatever else. Gratefully I turned this chore over to him and concentrated on trying to keep myself together. The last thing Kelly needed was to have to worry about us! This was all about her and how she would handle it; Bob and I would deal with us later. It would be a while before that happened.......

There had been a lot of telephoning back and forth to her dad, Lloyd and stepmother, Carol, in Texas and they visited as often as they could manage.. He counted on me to decipher some of the medical jargon and trusted my judgment, but couldn't help worrying about whether everything was being done that could be.

Recognizing and sharing his anguish, Bob and I kept him up-to-the minute informed. Once or twice, if Kelly had the phone in her room turned off, he called the nurses' station, and, as I relayed the latest information, the nurses indulgently ignored the time spent tying up their line.

We had been divorced since 1975, and, after the usual rocky beginnings, had ultimately arrived at a very comfortable friendship, some of which came from the fact that we had known each other since 9 th grade. For some time now it had been the pattern that whenever they came to town we would all go to dinner, a fact which surprised a lot of people, but our children accepted as the norm. One of them had once remarked "We had to go through hell to get here, but every thing worked out the way it was supposed to"

Now as he grappled with the reality of Kelly's illness we felt for him. They had only rediscovered each other a few months back, and now he was losing her.

Chapter Twelve

The oncology nurses and aides and all of the staff were fantastic! There was no aspect of care that was not delivered efficiently and caringly. They would stop by to see how Kelly was doing even if she wasn't on their team that day. They would call in to check on her when they were off duty. They encouraged us to call any time during the night to check on her progress when we weren't there. They made sure that her pain was alleviated, her fears comforted, and her personality left intact. They treated her like a person, shared stories about their families, and treated us like old friends, with plenty of hugs to go around. The oncology floor is an experience like nothing else! Friendships are formed when one person sees another crying softly near the elevator. More hugs, more tears, and a shared bond...not one we had asked for, but one that we embraced for each others' sake. We now learned that a support group had been formed and named in her honor, as a tribute to her courage and attitude. Yep, that's our Kelly!

In addition to the port in her chest, which delivered chemo systemically to all parts of her body, she elected to have another port, the Omaya Reservoir, implanted into her skull for the delivery of the chemo directly into the brain. The oncologist warned us that the best we could hope for was to alleviate the symptoms, and increase the quality of her life through pain relief, but the prognosis had not changed. We were still looking at a life span of 6-12 months, maybe slightly longer.

The treatment, chemo into the brain, and radiation to the neck and breast, was horrific, and most people didn't do well. We were pretty discouraged. The port in her skull would also provide access for removing some of the fluid which was accumulating too fast and causing the headaches. Ironically enough, her first chemo treatment had to be postponed because the fluid didn't build back up fast enough! This was not going to be easy! I had promised Kelly long ago, that if it seemed that the treatments were being done only because they could be and there was no hope of recovery, that I would tell her to stop. I wondered many times when that time should be and if it had come, but Kelly was capable of making her own decisions and her intent was clear.

"Mom I have no choice. I don't want to die. I'll do whatever I have to do to try to stay alive"

The next few months were swallowed up in treatments, side effects, and many trips to the emergency room, once for chest pain, and once when she couldn't swallow. Her dear friend and neighbor, a retired nurse, had been coming to help out and had brought her a baked sweet potato, hoping to tempt her appetite. Her weight had plummeted. From 126, she now was down to 90 pounds. She waged a constant battle with insomnia, incontinence, extreme fatigue, indigestion, depression, pain, and fear. We lost track of the Cat Scans and MRI's. We worried about this advance to the brain. Would it attack the optic nerve, rendering her sightless? Would she be subjected to seizures?

The mere act of traveling 15 miles each way to the treatment center was a Herculean feat for a body so ill. The pain prevented her from being able to sit up in the front seat, but lying down in the back seat caused unbearable nausea. At one point the radiation had been done daily for a six week period. The chemo now just totally wiped her out and very often she would just be admitted to the hospital for an overnight stay after the treatment. And, almost palpable, the ever-present realization that this most hated of all enemies could at any time attack the other breast or the uterus, or both.

There was never a lack of things to worry about. Worry and fear were our constant companions. We were now back and forth on a regular basis. Sometimes we could help Kelly, sometimes nothing could be done to help her, but we would go if we felt we could help John in any way. He was often called from work in the middle of the day, either to home, or, if she had already been taken by a neighbor to the hospital, he would go directly there. Life as they had known it had ceased to be, as had ours.

And after the nearly yearlong battle, the medical expenses and loss of income had taken their toll.

Chapter Thirteen

After one of his trips up there Mac had expressed some concern over their financial situation. "Mom, did you know that they were having a hard time?"

"No, I didn't, no one said anything"

"Kelly said she dropped a few hints, but apparently you didn't catch it"

" Guess not, I'm not good at subtle right now, you'd have to put a tattoo on my forehead, I guess. How bad is it?"

"Well, you know she had to close her business down"

"Of course she did. I just didn't think of it"

" John isn't able to get in any overtime, sometimes he barely gets in a full week at work"

" I know, we've gone up a couple of times to spend the day so that he could get to work. I just didn't t' realize things were that bad"

" Well, there's a house payment, the camper, and the usual things, credit cards, and stuff and the van has over 100,000 miles on it and needs repair. I think they've gotten behind. I have an idea"

"Okay, what is it?"

" I was thinking that if the entire family would commit a certain amount every month, at the same time, then that would be a definite amount that they could count on, and we could help out till things get better"

This wasn't idle chatter, he had already contacted a couple of members of the family, and had purchased several cards, with several different messages, and had addressed and stamped the envelopes for each. I was so proud of him!

Eventually Kelly would collect on a disability policy they had taken out and things would ease up. Their financial advisor had told them, a long time back, that a disability policy was one of the wisest investments working people can make, and her words would prove to be prophetic.

When we were home, we wanted to be up there, and when we were up there things piled up at home. Our social life was gone, our house was a mess, mail piled up, all but the most crucial things were ignored. We just couldn't concentrate on anything. Often I would take unfinished work, such as mending, or bills to be paid, and do these things in the car as we traveled back and forth. Our medical checkups were ignored and we willed ourselves to stay well. Unfortunately, on one planned weekend, our will didn't hold out. Bob had a sore throat and I questioned the advisability of his making the trip with me. Feeling that Kelly and John both needed him, he decided to ignore the whole thing and go anyway.

I finally convinced him to visit our family doctor first and if he got his okay I wouldn't argue the point. His assistant, a very capable Nurse Practitioner, put it this way"You're already on medication,

MOM, I FOUND A LUMP

you're doing everything you should be doing, and I know if it were my daughter, I'd be going too. Just take good care, and don't be foolish" He wore a precautionary mask to prevent Kelly (or anyone else) from being infected by him, and got his reward when he heard her weak little voice whispering "I'm so glad you're here"

Chapter Fourteen

" Mom, I know you think I'm in denial, but I really do think I'm going to beat this. I know my prognosis, but I don't accept it. I think I will be a miracle patient and will beat the odds and live"

" I hope you will, honey, you know I hope you will. I hope you will prove the doctor wrong and I'm sure he hopes so too. You are on every prayer list there is. "

" I don't know why this happened. I think God wanted to get my attention"

" I think He's got it!"

" I don't know what He has in mind for me, but I really think I am meant to live"

" No one wants that more than I do"

"Mom, I just hit bottom and I put myself in His hands and said ' Jesus, take my life and do what you will with it' and such a feeling of peace and calm came over me. It's like I have a direct line to Him at all times. It's the most wonderful thing. I can't describe it, but I'm not afraid. I put my trust in Him"

Now I took her little, frail hand in mine and spoke the unspoken, the unspeakable.

"Kelly, sweetie, I promised you long ago that I wouldn't let you be tortured. If you felt that God was ready for you, could you accept it?

You know once Rev. Adams told us that at the moment of death, Jesus comes down and wraps his arms around us and takes us up with Him. Isn't that a beautiful explanation?"

"I'm not ready to die. I'm going to fight. I have a husband and children, and I'm not ready to leave yet. Whatever my purpose in life is, I haven't learned yet, but I believe He has something in store for me"

Although Kelly had been baptized as a child, we had not been a particularly religious family and certainly had never had a conversation like this before! I would remember it later……………..

The gifts kept coming, the cards kept coming, the flowers kept coming. The staff all made a pet of her and she became interested in their lives outside the hospital, their children, their hobbies. Her former boss sent a donation to the cancer society, a touching gift which brought tears to her eyes. And there were some who never called. They will be remembered also. Kelly and I talked about this a lot.

"Mom, I don't understand. They were supposed to be such good friends. Why wouldn't they call to see how John is doing? I have all kinds of people taking care of me, but John never gets a break. Couldn't they at least invite him out for a beer or something? They go back 20 years!"

"Honey, we don't choose our friends for what they can do for us, but when people act like this, it tells you something. Let it go! You have so many nice friends now, true friends, forget the others. They have sent you a message. Move on!"

Two neighbors, Carol and Annette, had noticed things going on at the house and had asked to be allowed to help out! Both devout Christians, they had a hand in Kelly's renewed spirituality, sharing cassette tapes, stories, Bible lessons. Kelly soaked it all up eagerly. These two very special ladies will also be remembered for the day when, after Kelly lamented that she was tired of bed baths and would "kill for a shower", the two of them stripped down, along with Kelly, and held her up, showered her, and shampooed her hair. What a gift!

Her friends, Tammy(two Tammy's) and Samantha, and Carlotta were never far away. They did so many nice things that I could list here and the list would be long, but most of all they gave her love. Sam and Kelly had been friends since grade school and she had always been a favorite of mine. Very willing to take her punishment after indulging in some teenage misbehavior or other, I always felt a kinship with this other Aries person. She and Kelly had remained close throughout the years. Always very bright, Sam was now vice-president of a bank, and lived with her husband and young son on the West Coast, but came over to help as often as possible and kept in touch. Tammy was there for both John and Kelly; their families had camped together when Kelly was able. Another Tammy, a former co-worker, also made herself available to help. Carlotta was part of Kelly's life every day, in every way. Suddenly Kelly had many "sisters"

With all of the things that were being done for them, the responsibility for the children, the house, the bills, getting back and forth to the hospital on his lunch hour, getting up at night when Kelly was home....all fell to John. Dear sweet John, who got up each morning and dealt with packing lunches, getting breakfast, getting both kids ready, driving one to school and one to the babysitter, then putting in his day at work. ...hopefully uninterrupted by a crisis. These came fairly frequently and he would have to leave to take care of them. Once off work, it was pick up the kids and begin the 4 hour marathon of dinner, baths, playtime, quality time, homework, bedtime, taking care of Kelly, the never-ending laundry, and whatever else came up. Often he wouldn't get to eat until 10 or so and sometimes he fell asleep without eating. We were all worried about him. We would call to check on him in between our trips, and we wondered how long he would be able to keep going. He was exhausted and worried and depressed also, and there was no medicine for him! Finally he went to his boss and said, simply "I need a week off or I'm going to crack"

At last, a brief-all-too-short-but much-welcomed respite for the caregiver! He showed his love for Kelly in a million little ways and he never wavered....but he needed rest.

Were things ideal? Absolutely not. Patience wore thin, there were spats, and sometimes things were said that caused hurt feelings. Everyone was worried, exhausted, and John was angry.

"Mom, I hope someday that John will find the Christian faith that I have, but right now he's just kind of mad and doesn't want to hear about God"

" He's entitled! You know that's not uncommon. I don't have the faith that you have, either, Kelly"

"I can't describe it, I'm just so thankful for Annette and Carol. They help me with my Bible lessons, and I listen to tapes when I can't read or do anything else.

They've been like sisters to me"

As I listened to her, my mind wandered off a little. Why wouldn't someone in John's position be a little angry? Maybe I was too, but I just couldn't let myself go there. I had been there before, but this was a different "ballgame" We never had a chance to be caregivers to Scott.

Chapter Fifteen
Practicalities and Realities

I have watched with slight skepticism as some celebrities are lauded for being there every day and doing little things for their loved ones, and I have often thought" Sure, you do, but you have household help. What about the single parent who's got a couple of kids at home, and simply can't get to the hospital?"

How does a caregiver cope with the loss of sleep, worry over the loss of salary, worry about home or car repairs that simply can't be made?

When you're too tired to feel your own back, where do you find the strength to rub someone else's back .....lovingly...at 3 a.m., after changing the bedding?

When you want to give in to the grinding self pity, how do you come up with a believable" It's all right honey, I don't mind"?

Even with insurance supplements, even with household help, the job at hand is insurmountable. Who can help the caregiver come to grips with the dismal future while trying to provide a cheerful present?

If you're struggling every minute to keep the world the same for the person you most want to help, how do you prepare yourself to live in a world that has already, irrevocably changed forever?

Is the caregiver allowed to resent that extra trip to the store for a favorite food that might abate the chemo-induced nausea, when there has not been time for him /or her to eat? Is it unfair to calculate how far the budget is stretched by all The extras not covered by insurance?

Is it really awful to wish you could crawl into one of those hospital beds and push a call button for what you need?

I'm pretty sure that every family that has ever dealt with a major illness or death has dealt with these things as well.

This book is written to share the story of the fantastic support that we had and the family dynamics that allowed us to help each other. But it is also an acknowledgment of the realities of illness. You can't wish them away. You summon every bit of strength you have and when one of you falters, another gets you going again, and you do it for each other and you keep doing it and you keep doing it....and still feel guilty that it never seems enough.

Chapter Sixteen

"Mom, could you just come up for the day? I'm so bored, I can't read or watch TV. I just lie in the room all the time with the shades drawn, like a mole"

"When did you start doing that?"

"The ophthalmologist says the chemo is attacking my eyes"

"We're on the way"

The chemo, which is effective because it attacks the growing cancer cells, also attacks the new, healthy cells...the hair follicles and –alas—cells we need for sight.

Nothing could be done to improve this situation as long as Kelly was still on chemotherapy. We had bought her a sleep mask to use to shut out the strong lights in the hospital room, but she now wore it all the time. This was a flamboyant, leopardskin mask—-a treasure found after much searching—-at Frederick's of Hollywood, home of the most exotic of ladies lingerie.

Kelly laughed at that one, "Mom, I can't believe you took my 3 year old into that place!"

"Yep, she loved it; actually looked good in a couple of the outfits!"

"Mom!"

KIDDING!

A small smile, difficult to come by now. Kelly was depressed, bored, discouraged. She had been evaluated for physical therapy at home and they determined that she was not a candidate; she simply had nothing to work with.

They issued a walker, bedside commode, and all the other hospice trappings. Her friend, Carlotta, had helped her with the paperwork to shut down her accounting business, and she now helped her with this new paperwork..

In order to qualify for hospice, a patient has to be deemed" terminal", meaning that life expectancy is 6 months or less.

" Mom, I know I'm supposed to be terminal, but its still a horrible shock to see it stamped across my records"

How did I answer her? Did I answer her?

Could this really be happening? This once vital person, now barely able to see, trying to do as much of this paperwork as she could?

The last time we had had to fill out this many forms was back when Kelly and John applied to become foster parents. They had so much love to give, they decided to share it with some of the unfortunate, unloved kids out there.

One little girl came with cigarette burns on her body. Kelly was furious.

"Mom, do you believe I had to make a police report today because someone decided to abuse a poor little kid?"

Another came who gulped her bottle so fast that she subsequently threw up. I remarked that she acted as if she had to inhale it quickly, as is she thought there might not be any more. Quite right, Kelly said, the mother used to take off, and no one knew how often this child did get fed.

We solved the problem by making a very thick cereal feeding which she took through a cross-cut nipple, causing her to take much longer to eat, and so to feel satisfied when she did. Kelly was so proud when she was able to see this child eat without vomiting! There were many other little boys and girls who came into their care.

" Mom, they come so dirty, and in dirty clothes, if they even have any. The first thing I do is put them into a nice long bubble bath and wash their hair and their ears! They love it!"

We had been asked to give testimony as to the kind of parents they would be and responded that they would provide the kind of home that every child should have a right to expect. Sadly, many don't.

Things were underway for Kelly's disability to go through and not long after her white blood cell count dropped to 500, almost non-existent, and chemo had to be suspended.

And then....................REMISSION!. Things started looking up, she felt stronger, appetite improved, even felt strong enough to drive the short distance to take Anthony to school and go to the doctor by herself. MRI showed NO cancer cells. Boy, did we celebrate! Kelly said the doctor was surprised, but she wasn't.

"I told you I was going to do this"

August 2002

Typically Kelly, she used some of her strength to visit a terminally ill friend in the hospital.

"Mom, I wasn't sure if I could do it. I sat outside in the car for a long time, but John and I really wanted to be with him. We sat with him all night the night before he died, and we talked a lot and I really think I was able to help him"

And I remembered the conversation we had had so many months before. Of course she would do this. Where she found the strength we don't know, but that was Kelly.

She and Anthony came down for a weekend. Mac went up and got them and we had a fantastic time. While Meghan and Daddy enjoyed their one-on-one time at home, we had a weekend to remember, which included shopping and lunch like the old days, and family meals, and on Sunday, she came to our church with us.

Bob and I proudly got on stage with her and introduced her to the members of our church, who had all been praying for her, but some had not yet met her. Oh, it was great! We knew it wasn't a cure. We knew we would eventually lose her, we had always known that, but we hoped this remission would last a long time.

It lasted 4 months!

Chapter Seventeen

The type of cancer she had, "Carcinomatous meningitis" was diffuse, inflammatory, not like a solid tumor to be excised, more like it spread along the lining of the meninges, as if along the inside of a pipe. If eradicated from one area, it could still be clinging to the lining in some other area.

I wondered now, where was the "quality of life?" She was either in the hospital on IV morphine, or at home unable to control the unrelenting pain with oral medication. We talked about things.

"Mom, I don't want to die"

"Honey, I can't bear the thought of losing you, but I promised I wouldn't let you be tortured. Are you tired of fighting?"

" I have to fight, Mom, I don't have a choice. I want to live. I want to stay with John and the children"

Kelly and I had always been close, we had been friends as well as mother and daughter, and there was no subject that was taboo, ever, but this was brand new territory. What were the rules here? I couldn't bear the thought of life without her, but knowing that it was inevitable, I felt a need to prepare her, to make it easier for her, to help her to think that God was, indeed, waiting for her.

An aide came to the door, astutely surmised the situation, and said," Do you need a few minutes?"

" Yes, I need to talk to my Mom"

"I'll come back later". Thank you, whoever you were.....

"Mom, John and I have made out a will. I never thought I'd be doing that, but we had to get some things straightened out."

She then outlined all of the things she had planned.

"Are you telling me you don't want me to sing?" (I can't sing, not at all!)

" No, I don't want you to sing. Please! I want you to have a hell of a party, and I want you to make me a key lime pie"

On December 19, shortly after midnight, we received a call from John, saying that the doctor had called him, advising that they had found Kelly unresponsive, all indications being that she had suffered a CVA(stroke). He didn't know whether she would make it through the night. We were on the road within minutes, traveling the now too-familiar road. I hated every inch of the boring, colorless macadam of the turnpike. We had not been asleep long before the phone had rung, but were now wide awake, our nerves taut and our senses on alert for whatever may be ahead.

When we were about an hour away we realized that Bob had not eaten for several hours and his diet-controlled diabetes demanded that he eat on a regular basis. Not knowing what might be available at this hour we decided that we had no choice but to find an all-night place for a quick something for him. He ate something, he didn't know what and didn't know how it tasted, and I cried a lot.

The waitress, a thirtyish, stout brunette with an efficient manner and a noticeable Southern accent, stayed nearby and kept nervously looking our way, but was just too unsure whether to approach us or not. Every swallow of my hot chocolate was replaced, I think, with tears falling into the cup. I'm sure she thought that Bob and I were breaking up, or at the very least were having a very public problem. What a spectacle! Would make a good story for her to tell later. That's okay. I wasn't too pleased with her, either.. How could she be so cheerful and go on making hamburgers as if everything was the same? Didn't she know, couldn't she sense that the world had just turned over? Wasn't it obvious to everyone?

We arrived at the hospital around 4 a.m, surprised to find that the usually crowded parking lot now afforded us any spot of our choosing. Of course! This is a time when people come to visit only in the direst of circumstances! Hurrying through the bitter cold, wind and rain, we now had only to endure the final delay of security procedures before finally being where we could see and touch our daughter.

We sat by her bedside till that afternoon, and we were astounded at the numbers of people who came in to see her. People who had taken care of her, or who had heard about her. Nurses, aides, everyone, stood by her bedside crying, saying "We love her, we just can't lose her"

Bob and I spent the day giving and receiving hugs, and crying tears of gratitude, joy, sadness, and loss of hope. She had touched so many people, why did we have to lose her?

In the afternoon she rallied! It was determined that she had not suffered a stroke but had, instead, a serious imbalance of body electrolytes...sodium, potassium, and the others which keep the human body functioning. Once restored, Kelly improved to the point where she would be discharged on Monday, two days before Christmas.. Now we had a decision to make. There certainly wouldn't be much of a Christmas this year. Should we go home and take care of what we had left behind, and then come back? Should we try to make a Christmas for them, or just be there to baby-sit, if Kelly is still in the hospital and let her and John have Christmas Eve at the hospital, if that is all that they will have? We decided to do just that, and would return to Ft. Lauderdale late Christmas day, in time to spend the remainder of the Holiday with the rest of the family. Kelly came home on Monday, and difficult as it was, we now determined that, if this was to be their last Christmas, they should have it together, and we stayed home. We talked by phone, and it was evident that this would be her last Christmas. The doctor had let her come home, not because she was ready, but because he knew she had to.

After Christmas when Mac went to visit her, he found Kelly in pretty good spirits, but their discussion somehow turned to the funeral plans that she had made and the struggle she had been through.

"I don't know how someone could go through this without John"

Mac would later tell people that he believed that she meant exactly what she said. Not "someone like" her husband, but how could anyone make it through without her John.

Chapter Eighteen
The End of a Beautiful Life

On January 3rd, Kelly had another of these episodes. John was called and he advised us to get there as quickly as possible. Before we had gone 20 miles, she was gone.

So where are we now? "Doing okay", we say, but walking around with an unremitting ache, a wound that will never heal.

And remembering..........

Remembering the wonderful friends and neighbors, and people from our church, who made the 3 hour trip to be there at the funeral. Remembering how our strangely composite family came together. My former husband, Lloyd, came from Texas with his wife, Carol. Carol's son, Kent, came from Tennessee, stopping in Atlanta for Doug and they made the rest of the trip together. We all stayed at the same motel and kept each other company, and supported each other .

Remembering that the funeral service was "standing room only". One of her former co-workers even came on his lunch hour from work! Her picture atop the casket had to be removed. There were some, her brothers and her aunt among them, who just couldn't handle seeing the reminder of her once-lively face.

Remembering how the funeral director was so moved by the number of people and the obvious way Kelly had touched so many lives that she, too, began to weep, openly.

Remembering the people who came to the house after the funeral....and yes, I did make the key lime pie.

Lloyd asked me during this time, if I felt that Kelly had had the best of care, or did we do wrong by not moving her to another place. My reply was that Kelly was exactly where she needed to be. She was going to leave us, no matter what we did, that had already been decided by Someone Else. Kelly was right where she needed to be to have the best of medical care, family support, friends who loved her, neighbors who wanted to help, there was nothing more that could have been done for her.

She died close to those she loved, and ready to meet her Savior through her new found faith. She is at peace.

We are so grateful for having had Kelly. We are so privileged to have learned from her some of life's hardest lessons. I felt grateful and privileged to have brought Kelly into the world and to have been her mother for 43 years. And I felt grateful and privileged to have been able to help her when her time here was done.

But will I ever put a key lime pie in the refrigerator again without wanting to put a "tasting spoon" in it for her?

When I see Mothers and daughters shopping together, I feel deprived....and I sometimes go into the ladies room and cry.

Bob's conversations are peppered with "Kelly would have loved this" or "I wish we could show this to Kelly" We both still wake up in the night and half expect one of those I'm-lonely-I'm-bored-I'm-scared calls from her hospital bed.

We've done this before. We know what to do. We'll get through it.

We are watching John take hold of the lives of the children and he is doing so amazingly well, we are so proud of him! His life is still on hold, he knows he will be dedicated to them for many years to come, and he is ready for the challenge.

The children are amazingly balanced, and contented. They talk about Kelly and he helps them as much as he can. Loneliness is his companion, but he sees to the children first, always.

"Grandma, my Mommy is dead"

"I know, Meghan, I know"

" I miss her, she was my best friend"

"Mine, too, sweetie"

Anthony is still a little angry, but John is helping him work through it, and is getting some counseling for him, a wise move, we feel. John is instinctively making the right decisions and we help all we can. We are still a family.

We promised ourselves that we would try to be as brave as she was.

Seven weeks before she died, on the anniversary of Scott's death, Kelly sent me flowers, as she had done since 1989.

Five weeks before she died they made a trip to Georgia, to spend Thanksgiving with her brother, Doug. They would camp near where he lived, as they had done before, and he would join them there. Before leaving she went to her favorite meat market and stocked up on all of Doug's favorite cuts of meat to take to him. That was our Kelly. We don't know where the strength came from to do all of that. We do know that this trip, this time with Kelly, left Doug with the most cherished of memories, a true gift from a sister.

Was Kelly perfect? Of course not. Did she have faults and weaknesses? Of course she did, and as her mother, I usually was the first to know about them. But we all have faults and weaknesses; they don't define the person, they are only part of the total package. And what an extraordinary package she was....................

Here is the way we think Kelly would want to be remembered:

Keep her in your heart, keep her close

Enjoy the memories you cherish most

Life won't be the same from this day

Loving her has changed us all in some way

Yet her strength is there whenever we need it

Her lesson is there if only we heed it.

Open yourself, feel the courage displayed

We knew she'd be leaving; it was only delayed.

Acceptance is hard, but let's

Rejoice in what is true

Do remember :as you loved her, she also loved you.

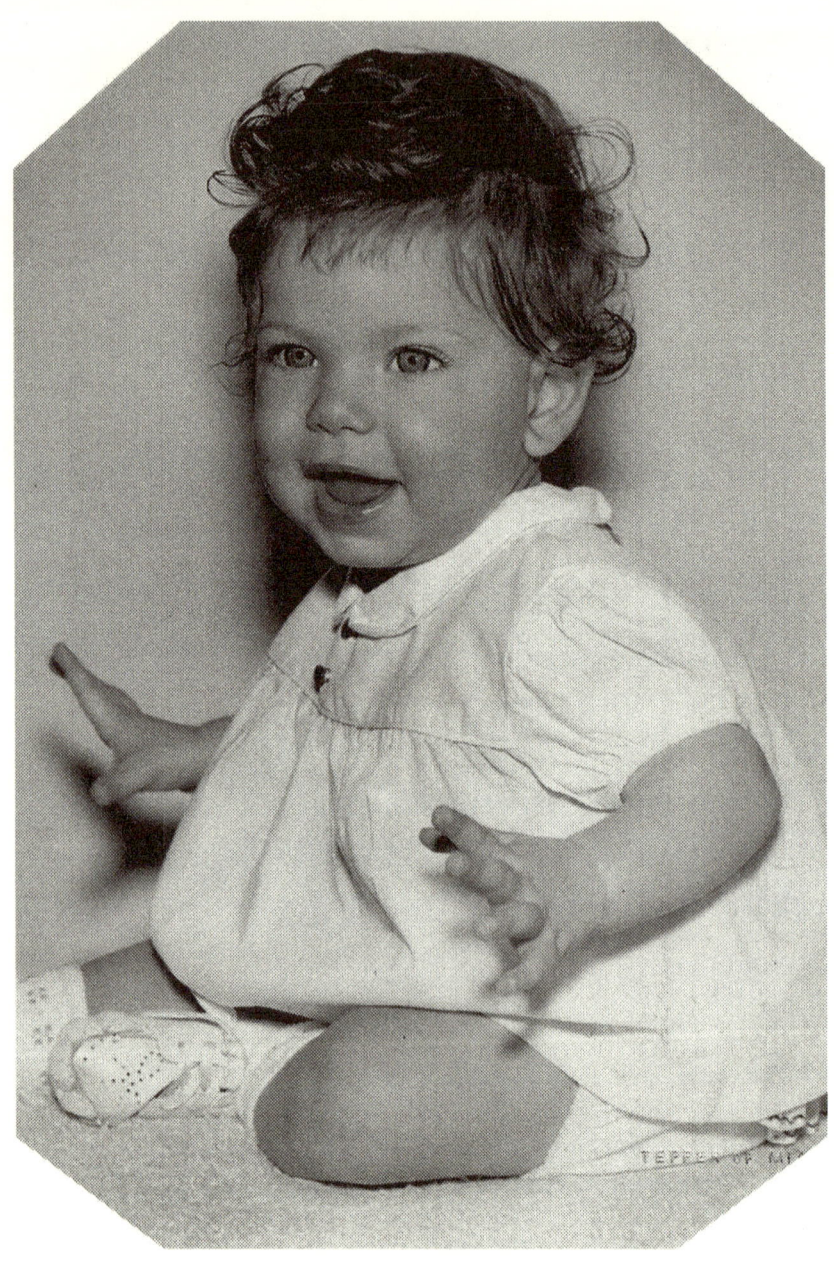

Kelly 5 mos. old

Kelly
Not quite 2

Kelly
Around age 4

Dec 1977
Clowning around with Aunt Kay

TEENAGE REBELLION

"There are rules", he said, "which cannot be ignored. We love you as we love one another, but you, in your newfound wisdom, must decide"

"Where will you be happier?", he asks this child he has adored.

"Is there a place for you to hide from the realities of the world?, they follow like your skin"

"I can't accept your rules", she said, "there is a me within"

"I know much more than you", says the stubborn tilt of her head "Perhaps, parents, you shall soon be as wise as I"

Perhaps....we've learned since we first saw you in your pink bed. We've learned to leave the door open and never say goodbye.

Dec. 1976
17½ years old

Kelly
7/7/1959 - 1/03/2003

KELLY IS TWENTY ONE!

Last month brought your birthday and now you're twenty one!
The number doesn't matter; the raising's long been done.

I've been so very proud of you, it's such a joy to see
The kind of loving person that you turned out to be.

You've been tender and supportive in your big sister role
And did whatever was needed to help keep this family whole.

There wasn't any money, we were sometimes overdrawn.
We met with every crisis from the roof down to the lawn.

We fought and cried and argued as we dealt with ups and downs
Talked and hugged and shared, and played and often laughed like
clowns.

We've found we like each other; we didn't have to wait
Till one of us had gone away, or till it was too late.

How very fortunate I am….what a beautiful blend
When you remind me, you're not just my daughter, you're my friend.

And now the time is coming for you to "leave the nest"
In fact the nest is moving, too, a little South and West.

Another new beginning, for now we'll live apart.
But still a part of each other's lives and still in each other's hearts.

Dedicated to Kelly, September, 1978, as she moved into her own
apartment.

Doug

Scott
4/30/64 - 11/12/89

Mac with Lexi

Bob

Grayce and Bob

Bob, Mac, Doug

WEDDING TOAST TO KELLY AND JOHN, 1990

A daughter fills a special place in your life
You tell each other secrets, far into the night.
    She's a child who later becomes a friend
And you get to know each other all over again.
    You comfort each other when things are at their worst
And run to share the good things with each other first.
    You prepare yourself to give her away
To that special guy she'll meet someday.
    You teach her all you know as the years go along
About being independent....but hopefully not too strong.
    About cooking and keeping house and budgeting and fashion
About loving and being loved and kindness and passion.
    She sees by your example how it all can come together
And you hope someday she'll find the same and it will last forever.
    Then one day she calls and says:"Mom,......Bob, I've met the
one!"
And you know she means it.....you can feel it through the phone.
    And when you meet this terrific guy who now becomes your son
It all falls into place somehow.....you know your job is done.
    It's all there in their faces.....everything is there for her.
You know you have no worries, for he will always care for her.
    So now it's time to party, there's really no more to say
It's time to toast and kiss and hug and have friends share this day.

Mr. & Mrs. Howard
Kelly and John on their wedding day in Colorado

Anthony and Meghan
2003

Kelly's stepmother, Carol and Dad, Lloyd

OOZIE BOOBIE BARBIE

Oozie Boobie Barbie's not doing well right now
Her scar makes her queasy and sleeping ain't easy
But she'll overcome it somehow.

Her mouth feels scalded and her head is getting balded
Yes, her hair is everywhere.
She takes what each day brings, tries to do the right thing
And tries not to despair.

She fights the good fight but the middle of the night
Brings pain and a new terror
Will the chemo be victorious? Oh, won't that be glorious?
There is no room for error.

Oozie-Boobie Barbie has learned about nutrition
Has taken quite an active role in improving her condition
She has friends who help her every single day
So she tries to use her energy in the most constructive way.

Her family adores her, helps in any way they may
For her hurt is their hurt; it's always been that way
A rough year is ahead for her our Oozie Boobie Queen
But she has hidden strengths in her, you haven't even seen.

A mastectomy looms, there's no doubt about it
She'll grieve for the breast but is prepared to live without it.
Oozie Boobie's a gutsy broad, and always was, we guess.
She intends to win this battle, and will accept no less.

She'll deal with the vomiting, the surgeries and scars
And each time she looks at her "Ken" she'll thank her lucky stars.
He'll take her hand and help her to plow through all the sorrows
She'll trade an Oozie Boobie for all of their tomorrows.

We sent Kelly a Barbie doll with long(past waist)
Curly, blonde hair, and this poem attached to it
When her wound was open and seeping.

SOME RANDOM THOUGHTS THAT MAY BE HELPFUL

People have said that I am very strong, I guess perhaps I am. I don't know. My response has always been" What choice is there?" It's not as if God calls and says "I'm thinking of taking your loved one tonight. What do you think?" And then you say, "Oh, no, I'd rather you wouldn't" When you get that phone call, you have NO CHOICE but to accept.

That is my theory. Perhaps those who can't accept end up drinking a lot or being hospitalized, I'm not sure. Maybe that is the difference. I do know that, seeing Kelly's bravery, I vowed to do no less. We had no chance to prepare for Scott's death as we did for Kelly's. I never asked for a reason because there was no explanation that could be good enough. Acceptance was my salvation, not trying to undo what was already done. This is about acceptance and communication, but it is not about what you can say. It's more about listening. I have never had any patience with people who made scenes at funeral homes, or worse, abandoned the families because they "couldn't take it". If ever there was a chance to be a good friend, this is it. Just BE THERE! No matter how well-intentioned, try to avoid the "call me if you need anything" You will not get that call.

How much more compassionate to come and just do! One day we were trying to pack some extra things into the bag and get everything into the car, for Kelly had taken a bad turn, and we had to get there fast. Our neighbor came, and, seeing that we were in no shape to do it, packed everything up and got us ready.

After the last particularly dispirited Christmas, our decorations were still up in January. Some friends came, and seeing them, helped us to box everything up and get them into the attic. Find things to do! Go to the store, scrub the bathroom, do some laundry, take a kid out for awhile. Make phone calls, baby-sit. Any little thing that you can do is that much stress removed from family members who just can't get it together right now.

Remember that you can talk to your loved one about things. I am so grateful that Kelly and I had some times that, unfortunately, I never had with Scott. My faith was renewed in knowing that Kelly died secure in her place with her Savior and she went to him, not because she wanted to leave this earth, but joyfully, nonetheless.

Remember that there are other family members who need you! My Scott died just before Thanksgiving and I knew that if I went to pieces Thanksgiving, and maybe Christmas, would forevermore be times to dread.

Count your blessings.......and let your loved ones know that you are. Every day is a gift. There were many more conversations that I have not shared in this book......but you get the idea.............................

ABOUT THE AUTHOR

The author, Grayce Upshaw, has been writing since adolescence. Formerly a newspaper reporter in the Cape Canaveral area, her writings have included Women's' page features, a daily column, and an abundance of poetry. This is her first novel.

During her daughter's illness, Grayce found that being an R.N.(retired) was a mixed blessing. There were times, she said, when knowing too much was not an advantage.

Grayce is the mother of four children. Her two surviving sons, Mac and Doug, live in Plantation, Florida, and Acworth, Georgia. She is the grandmother of 11 children and lives with her husband, Bob, in Ft. Lauderdale, Florida.

They love to dance, play cards and board games and have a very busy social life. Both are very active in their church, the Worship Center in Plantation, Florida, where Grayce is Team Leader for the Bereavement/Grief committee.

Grayce continues to write, does a monthly column for her condo association, and is on their hospitality committee. She and Bob also spend as much time as possible with their sons, and son-in-law, John, and Anthony (now 8) and Meghan (now 5)

Author, Grayce Upshaw

You may contact the author for information
On how to obtain additional copies of this book
@(954) 452-3021.
Author is available to speak to your group
Your comments are welcome.
Thanks,
Grayce.